FRAGMENTS OF US

Navya Kapoor

Made with ❤ on the BookLeaf Publishing Platform
www.bookleafpub.in
www.bookleafpub.com

*To my family, whose support and encouragement
inspired me to write this book.*

Acknowledgement

I would like to express my heartfelt gratitude to BookLeaf Publishing for providing me with the opportunity to participate in the '21 Day Writing Challenge'. This journey has tickled my creative bones and allowed me to connect with my inner poet. Their constant support has been invaluable in bringing this book to life.

I am also grateful to my family whose unwavering support has fueled my love for writing. Your encouragement has been my anchor, inspiring me to discover the depths of my voice. Thank you for always standing by my side. This collection is a testament to the love and faith of those around me, and I dedicate it to everyone who has inspired me along the way. Thank you for being a part of this beautiful endeavour.

Preface

One question has always lingered in my mind whenever I read a poem: *Why does poetry resonate with so many people?* After all, we live vastly different lives, shaped by unique experiences. Realistically, it should be impossible for thousands to see themselves reflected in a single piece of poetry. Yet, as I grew older, I slowly began to find the answer. Poetry, I realized, is a mirror that reflects the shared essence of humanity—a universal thread connecting us all, even amidst our individuality.

The title of this collection reflects the process of writing and reading poetry itself. Each piece is a fragment of my own thoughts and reflections, offered in the hope that you, the reader, will glimpse something of yourself within these words. After all, poetry is like a mirror, and in these verses, you might catch a reflection of your thoughts and emotions—sometimes familiar, sometimes surprising, but always meaningful. None of us are complete on our own. We are shaped by those we encounter, the lives we touch, and are touched by, and the lessons we learn along the way.

In these verses, you will encounter the unyielding spirit of generations grappling with tradition and progress, the wistful echoes of imaginary friends left behind in childhood, and the profound question of whether we truly live or merely exist. These poems invite you to find joy in fleeting moments while critiquing outdated norms we continue to follow.

The silent sacrifices of mothers are honoured in "Silent Architects", and the journey of life is celebrated in "Take Your Time." Simple pleasures, like sipping hot chocolate are explored, while hope acts as a compass in "Strength of Hope". Love, in its myriad forms—tailored, distant, or lost—resonates throughout these pages.

The collection contemplates the hollowness of wealth, the courage to break free from societal checklists, and the resilience needed to face the uncertain realities of life. As you turn these pages, you'll reflect on the interplay of light and shadow, the scars and triumphs that define us, and the beauty in embracing life's impermanence.

May this collection offer you words and space to reflect, feel, and connect. In embracing our fragments, we begin to see the beauty of the whole. Welcome to *Fragments of Us*—a collection of poetry that invites you to piece together your narrative, one fragment at a time.

MY IMAGINARY FRIEND

Do you remember the time gone by?
When we were allies walking side by side,
Sharing our highs and lows, together we
could jest,
Even in silence, we were different from the
rest.

You carried a light in you when the
perspective was new,
When the courage to be kind could be only
found in few.

Your presence wasn't rare, even in thin air,
When a million questions swarmed my mind,
you always seemed to care.

But I grew up with responsibilities so clear,
You said, "Change is constant; there is
nothing to fear."
I took this advice, but left you behind at the
end,
When others said you were just an imaginary
friend.

Years have passed, yet my heart has kept your
memory alive,
As I set out to explore life's complex hive.
You're a part of my childhood I chose to
forget,
To face the realities that put me to test.

GENERATIONS

A brand-new generation is on a new journey
to embark,
Yet, "A petulant band of miscreants" is
society's constant remark.
We demand the freedom to make a choice,
only to be denied,
Is embracing the symphony of life, a choice so
vile?

Losing the chance to express, when appeasing
society becomes a quest,
How can one be creative when the world
demands a sincerity test?
Is that all to life— a puppet confined by
conventions?

The best of poets are unbound by embracing
their creative intentions.

We reach for the stars and embrace warmth
that fills our heart,
We work hard in life only to revel in the joys
of its every part,
We dream, we fall, and we rise again, crafting
new stories at the end,
Creating a legacy of hope where dreams can
transcend.

DO WE LIVE OR EXIST?

Do we live or merely exist?
Bogus question, don't you think?
Paper thin is our resolve to resist,
In a world of cruelty where only rules can
persist.

Do we live or merely exist?
To earn bread and butter is all we can think.
To work for joy may seem like an alien
concept to heed,
When grinding for success is a tested formula
indeed.

Do we live, or merely exist?
When life's simple joys are hard to resist,
Should we feel guilty for chasing our light,
When passion invites us to walk on a path so
bright?

MY REASON TO SMILE

Do I have many reasons to smile?
As I seek control over the whirlwind of my
mind,
It's easy to spot what is lacking in life
And forget the joys that gave me memorable
times.

Do I have many reasons to smile?
When I strive hard to make most out of life,
Yet behind the curtain when soft words
chime,
They embrace me with love and kindness
every time!

Do I have many reasons to smile?
Yes, I find them in fleeting moments all the
time.
When hope becomes my compass and guide,
I uncover the beauty that no one can hide.

MODERN LOVE STORIES

Love stories as old as time
Can never compel me to change my mind.
Engraved in stone, they may age each day,
But their control cannot sway me away.

Bricks and bones may tell the truth,
But they cannot change the outlook of youth.
We can choose our groom and bride with
pride,
And never immolate wives when their
husbands die.

We are no longer bound by ancient lore;
Mutual respect—Is it too much to ask for?
A pair follows the rules of the foundation laid,
Great love stories are never built in a day.

SILENT ARCHITECTS

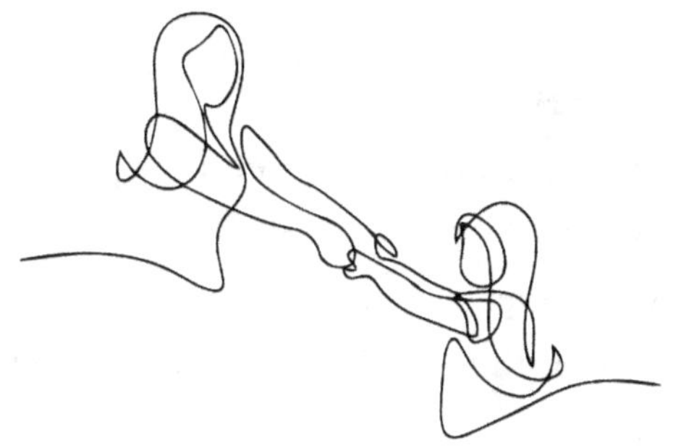

Taken for granted are our mothers,
When it may seem like they are unlike any
others.
A thousand poems have been written to
glorify their strength,
But very few are the ones who stop to relent.
They walk a path to build a generation,
Only to drink the bitter syrup of separation.

They are the silent architects of our life's
progress,
Weaving hopes and dreams for our success.
What happens to them? Is it their identity
they lose?
Do we celebrate the sacrifice or mourn the
identity they were made to refuse?

TAKE YOUR TIME

Take your time!
The world is riddled with questions
everywhere.
Pick your side!
The train of life could take you anywhere.
Stay alert!
Trouble can strike from any lair.
Don't be hurt!
When good fortune lies for you somewhere.
It's time to embrace!
Life's journey is a daring affair.
Even when your path twists and roads wear,
Your dreams will blossom when you bravely
dare.

WHAT OTHERS THINK

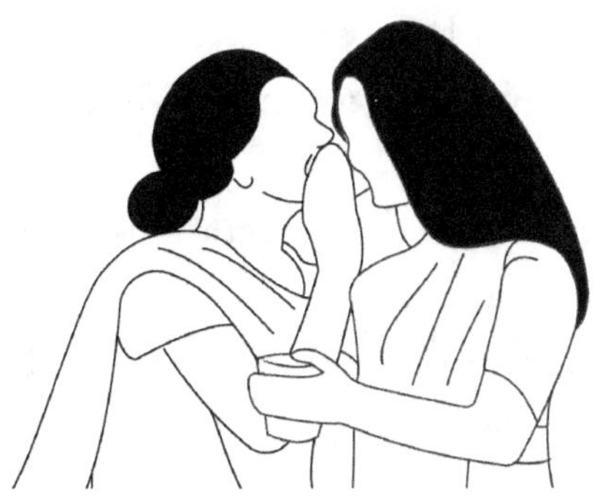

Facing the crowd, each step measured,
Tough endeavours of life are meant to be
treasured.
But a whisper lingers here, and a judgment
looms there.
What will others think? Is it truly fair to care?

Embrace your flaws to escape from society's
claws.
There is more to life than adhering to
unspoken laws.

'Abide by the rules, wrapped up in the fabric
of pride,
Or be detested by others in life's tragic ride.'

You pin your hope on the voice unseen.
Is it easy to accept when the whispers are
mean?
You never meet the expectations, even when
there's credence,
Will others accept your story when they
demand evidence?

Forget about others; just wait and see.
A strength within you is setting you free.
Who is like you, so unique to express?
You are much more than the ones you
impress.

HOT CHOCOLATE

This is a cup of hot chocolate,
Warmth infused in the perfect cup of cocoa,
A chocolaty cup of comfort to heal the soul,
A companion during winter, a Christmas
delight!
With a book by the fireplace, it's a companion
on an ideal night.

When a sore throat and common cold clouds
your thoughts,
A sip of hot cocoa becomes sweet medicine
for the heart.
A warm hug on cold days, a rare present,
Precious when we savor small things, bringing
a cuddly presence.
Marshmallows and whipped cream are
prescribed together as a perfect pair,
They melt together to create a tasty treasure
to share.

A cup of hot chocolate can be one's secret best friend.
A sweet fountain of comfort— may its warmth never end!

STRENGTH OF HOPE

Once upon a time, you dreamed a dream,
To embrace hope's ephemeral stream.
A temporary gleam that creates huge ripples,
Followers of such a path aren't always
redeemed.

They embark on a long journey where they
learn to grow,
Following a distant dream's path can often be
slow.
Resilience to rise and fall is a skill to hone,
For not every path will pave lasting
milestones.

So hold your breath for a journey so long,
It will test your resilience, but you must stay
strong!

Hope's temporary, but your efforts always
hold weight,
The fruits of hard work will always create a
sincere song.

TAILORED LOVE

Tailored love, this is us,
Walking a new path on this day.
Making faith forgettable,
Choosing a corrupt life, come what may.
Chasing dreams, as it may seem,
Taking unknown paths to test faith.
Even if we fail to reach our dream,
Tailored love will still pave the way.

LONG DISTANCE

Long distance, a new sentence,
Making its way through past tense.
Repentance, say old friends,
Does this journey have to end?
Making sense, present tense,
Texting is the new norm; hence,
Friendship dense, makes perfect sense,
All we need is a change of lens.

Long distance, love we send,
Through pixels and words, we defend.
Boundless and timeless, till the end,
Long-distance friends, forever penned.

LOST FRIEND

I still remember this old friend of mine,
As I live days with her thoughts, taking me
back in time.
A reserved soul, I met her when she was
sitting alone,
Eccentric role, her eyes hid some wisdom
unknown.

A woman of few words, yet much to convey,
A perceptive soul, never swayed by cruelty's
play.
She fought her demons with a unique aim in
her heart,
I found her ways unconventional, but still
played my part.

Bound by friendships, there were
expectations at stake,
Some exceptional conditions for a bond to
make.

But I fell short, did not live up to the
expectations,
I apologised for my faults, but maybe strength
didn't lie in our foundation.

She wanted to be heard, not told—a
challenging vision,
While I was stuck in a saviour complex, fixing
others was a mission.
What is poetry, if not a reservoir of friendship
lost?
I expressed my buried thoughts, but what was
the cost?

Did I write this poem to belittle a friend of
the past?
Or to honour the bittersweet memories that
didn't last?
Ironic, because this was a friendship I wanted
to cherish till the end,
Maybe I know the answer, as I'm still left with
residues of regret.

DOES WEALTH MEASURE GOOD?

A life of opulence is an enticing deal,
But there's more to the bargain than what
most see.
When worms of deceit wriggle in every story
The wealthy bask in their frivolous glory.

The sincere toil hard, putting their ambition
to test,
They take the long road, not often desired by
the rest.
Is the other path fair, built on the toil of
those you claim as kin?
Is it truly a fair win, when the gold you gain
leaves you empty within?

Riches glitter, but they tarnish with time,
The bonds you forsake once felt sublime.
In the end, will you remember the cruel game
you played?
Or take comfort in the innocent times that
never stayed?

What value does gold hold when it's the heart
it divides?
Shattering years of trust when love subsides.
Did you ever ponder the path you chose?
Without endless greed in your eyes, we could
have been close.

TAKE A BREAK

You've been running for so long; it's alright to take a break,
Relish a cup of coffee, and maybe also a slice of cake.
Let the warmth of this moment soothe your mind,
A relaxing break isn't always easy to find.

Savour the sweetness and the stillness in the air,
It's alright to recharge, no need to compare.
Take this time to rest and reflect,
Moments of silence are precious to collect.

RESERVOIR

My mind is a reservoir in its prime,
It helps me weave poetry every time.
I grasp some knowledge and store it inside,
There is much to learn and less to hide.

Thoughts run free, branching out like a tree,
Ideas are leaves, preserved in all we see.
Words become fruits, ripe and meaningful,
Each one is unique and so beautiful.

Dig into the roots of wisdom's soil,
Growth by efforts of curiosity's toil.
This reservoir is endless, vast, and true,
Holds dreams anew, with much to pursue.

SLOTH

Meaning making, a tough job,
When the interpreter is a sloth.
Condescending, these words may seem,
When putting in effort feels extreme.
Good men often procrastinate,
With no choice but to validate.
They tread the line, unsure, unsure,
From subtle meaning to obscure.
The weight of thought can be a hefty toll,
Except when understanding takes control.
Meaning blooms, though it may be late,
A patient heart will find its fate.
So the sloth may soar one day,
When its efforts lead the right way.

UNCERTAIN REALITY

One can always run fast and still come last,
Distracted by a greedy fire.
One can always hone his craft and still fall
short,
Becoming a needy liar.

One can always sing aloud and still be
unheard,
Drowned by the noise of a choir.
One can always speak the truth and still be
blurred,
Entangled in webs that conspire.

One can always dream big and still feel small,
Lost in the maze of desire.
An uncertain future, one can see and do all,
Yet still find themselves on an ambitious pyre.

WHAT THE HEART WANTS

What the heart wants is an everlasting bond,
I'll call out to fate, but will it always respond?
I like to live in reality, not with unrealistic
stories told,
But will it truly hurt to ask for more?
Someone who lives with cracks but embraces
the light within their heart,
As I learn to walk through storms and play an
integral part.
Someone who dreams, yet keeps their feet on
earth, steady and secure,
Is it too much to hope for love that's honest,
deep, and pure?

I'm fine if it's not true; I don't need a prince
on a gallant steed,
Just someone who could at least seldom meet
my heart's need.
Can I whisper the wish in my heart to the
stars above,
For a partner who can at least spare some
moments of love?
If fate listens closely, perhaps it will see
The beauty of someone as flawed as me.

YOU'RE BEAUTIFUL

Look in the mirror, you're beautiful,
You played your role so well, so dutiful.

We only spend few years with eyes youthful,
But your smile gleamed with grace, so
truthful.

Though you faced some circumstances with a
smile, so rueful,
Your heart and soul always remained kind and
fruitful.

Though time leaves lines on your face, so
beautiful,
It's a testament to your story, a life so
bountiful.

GUILTY ENVY

We are only humans; we are all just the same,
Jars of shared emotions, with different names.
We experience envy and jealousy alike,
As the ball of negativity doesn't take long to
strike.

Does this make us bad, when we all feel these
pangs?
Though calming the river of envy is always in
our hands.
The journey is not over, as we learn to
celebrate the gain of others,
Do not become a stranger, and learn to accept
success in different colours.

REALITY

"Live in reality," people often say;
"Don't live on a cloud, or be swept away!"

Work smart, but toil hard,
 Yet do not expect too much regard.

Stay alert, always on guard,
Regardless, you'll face blame and disregard.

You have standards? What a shame!
Flawed people are all the same.

It's easy to point fingers, to quickly accuse,
With distorted beliefs and broken views.

Reality is hard, and it's tough to thrive alone,
But with slow and steady steps, you'll find
your way home.

I BELIEVE

Years went by, harbouring doubt in my heart,
"I'm not good enough" – words I carried from
the start.
They held me back; I couldn't bring myself to
reconsider,
I had no choice, believing I could dream no
bigger.

But the changing tide brought gifts to impart,
Life taught me to embrace every chance from
the start.
Embracing risk can be the first step of
growth;
Comfort and risk, we can't have them both.

Whispers of failure fade with time,
Leaving pages empty for a new start, so
sublime.
Now I realise, maybe it isn't too late
To rewrite the story and change my fate.

COURAGE

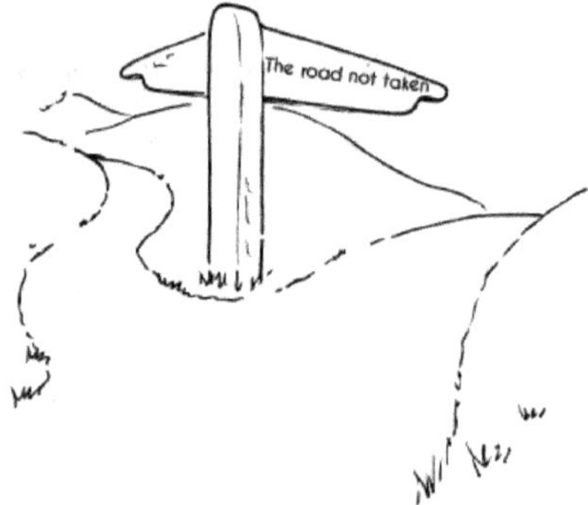

It's the time, the time to decide,
Will you be all alone, or will you take life in
stride?
Do you have the courage to be yourself today?
To do your best and put your talent on
display?

It's the time, the time to decide,
Will you be all alone, or embrace those you
like?
Do you have the courage to profess your love
today?
To be honest and let your soul sway?

It's the time, the time to decide,
Will you be all alone, or let cruelty slide?
Do you have the courage to speak up for
yourself today?
To rise above self-doubt and keep fear at bay?

It's the time, the time to decide,
Will you live in shadows, or let your spirit
ignite?
Do you have the power to embrace new
beginnings today?
To embrace the light within and leave fear at
bay?

A TICK ON THE CHECKLIST

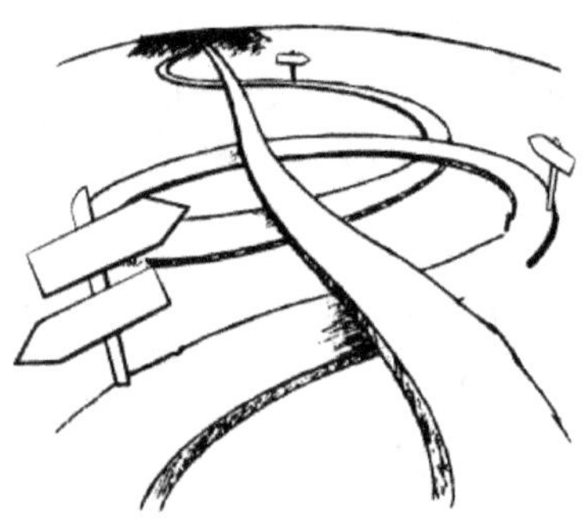

A tick on the checklist is all I see,
Not a choice to define what I can be.
I wake up with the building blocks of destiny,
Wearing the mantle of a forged legacy.
Complete schooling by 18, a degree by 22,
Settle your career by 26- this is all you can do.
They say it's your fate to get married by 28,
Is the timing of love so easy to dictate?
Tick, tick, tick— every box to conform,
But can I follow dreams that are not the
norm?

Can a pleaser not stray, to carve a journey of
her own?
Career and marriage should not be a box to
tick,
But a choice of heart, a journey that will stick.
So give me a chance to dream, stumble, and
rise,
To carve my own path and become wise.

SUCCESS

Experience days of toil after seeds are sown,
Through storms and trials, the roots are
grown.
A fleeting whisper of encouragement is a rare
grace,
Until success unveils its radiant face.
Even with shadows of doubt, courage persists,
Chasing the horizon, where dreams insist.
Every drop of sweat becomes a story untold,
As life blooms with success and confidence
so bold.

DISTRACTED

Don't be distracted, it's your life,
Learn to take everything with a stride.
Stay calm and focus on your work,
A patient present will give you future perks.

Don't be distracted, it's your time,
Work towards your goal while you're in your prime.
There is no age limit to learn, but many opportunities to miss,
So embrace every chance to grow, what can be better than this?

Don't be distracted, it's your way,
Shape your destiny with effort each day.
With some determination and fire in your
heart,
You'll sincerely achieve your dreams and play
your part.

COLD NIGHT

This is the night, hold on tight,
Turn up the heater; it's cold outside.
Brew your coffee, stay inside,
Watch the snowfall and enjoy your night.

Wrap yourself in a blanket warm,
A safe haven from the winter's storm.
Sip your coffee, feel the warmth and glow,
Let the night drift by, cozy and slow.

The ones outside may experience frost bite,
But you lie safely under a warm blanket
tonight.
The beauty of snowfall is a chilly delight,
When you're sheltered with comfort every
night.

REFLECTIONS OF DESTINY

Look at me, are you happy with your destiny?
Just wait and see; you'll come running back to
me.
Did you get a taste of the medicine by now?
You were always so harsh and refused to back
down.
Look at me, are you content with a fantasy?
Just wait and see; reality may bring clarity.
Did you squander your money on material
pursuits?
Are you ready to change and reconnect with
your roots?

Look at me, are you satisfied with your
memories?
Just wait and see; hard work can breathe life
into reveries.
Did you waste your time in a bubble of
daydreams?
Or did you strive to weave them into reality's
streams?
Look at me, are you happy with your destiny?
Just wait and see; peace lies in authenticity.
Did you let the world silence your inner
voice?
Or did you rise above and make your choice?
Look at me, you're more capable than you
think.
Just wait and see; your motivation's closer
than a blink.

ECHOES OF FUTURE

The book of every life turns an integral page,
Where the leaving mother's nest marks an
essential phase.
Children spread their wings to soar in sky,
As parents let them go, teaching them to fly.
They leave their home, yet they are never too
far,
As the memories and values once imbibed
stay where they are
They set out to find love and create a family
of their own,
But some people still miss the warmth of
comfort once known.

I've reached this stage too; I must make
choices in life,
Dreaming of a balance between career and
personal strife.
But there are still doubts in my mind, will the
journey be kind?
Will I be able to ask for support to ease my
mind?
When I've always had someone to rely on,
someone to care,
Will it be easy to walk on my own, facing the
dare?
I'll admit- the road ahead is scary, uncertain,
and new,
As I stumble forward without the support of
my crew.
But I'll take a deep breath and give a chance
to this new road,
As I'll do my best to embrace this
adventurous code.

CHANGE

We all grow up; it's a chapter of life,
But we still live through the blurry lens of
time.
When we're happy, time passes by like a gust
of wind,
But when we struggle to soar, time isn't so
kind.

We all change; it's our destiny to create.
With the crown of responsibilities, we
attempt to change our fate.
In the whirlwind of chaos, we find the
strength to fight,
Learning to look through a storm and chase a
distant light.

We all change but still hold on to a bygone
phase,
With memories of childhood—those carefree
days.
The grip of nostalgia is strong and tight,
Living in comfort when days felt just right.

But life doesn't wait for anyone, as it should,
Demanding growth, shifting the land where
we once stood.
Seasons change, and new chapters unfold,
Priorities shift, as the past grows old.

We all grow up; it's a part of the ride.
We embrace new roles with life's changing
tide.

DREAMS OF A CHILD

A child dreams of a future so bright,
Where he can be like anyone at sight.
With a mind like a magnet, to attract
attention,
And an optimistic soul with endless
retention.

From astronaut to doctor, and teacher at bay,
His choice of career can change every day.
Not held back by the inhibitions of the world,
He dreams to soar high in life like a bird.

Even after years his curiosity burns and heart
beats fast,
He knows this journey shouldn't be blurred
by the past.
When every success story whispers tales in his
ears,
It fills him with hope, not jealousy and fear.

Some lessons and trials make him strong,
Giving him confidence to see where he
belongs.
A world he carves, to make his dreams a
reality,
With faith in his vision and hopeful clarity.
The child can become an adult with a vision
so clear,
Without self-doubt, a path free of fear.
So allow him to fuel his dreams and aspire,
To build a bright future, fueled by desire.

REDEFINING THE WARRIOR

I looked at the 'warrior'; she had a strong grip on life,
Expecting to go on a timeless journey for a long time.
Her roots had been harvesting some silent thorns for years,
Shadowed resentments no one dared to bear or hear.

She fought for long, weaving tales in the
wrinkles of her face,
As others contemplated her strength to win
the tumultuous race.
When the warrior redefines strength, even
fortune rethinks its role,
Carving a safe future for those resolute
enough to grow old.

But what about the ones who never stay to
experience more tales of life?
Is it right to blame someone for losing an
uncertain fight?
Do others really 'lose' by not harnessing their
strength?
Or is it not a war with winners announced at
the end?

I promised the tale of a warrior, but let's
change some trends.
Let's turn the warrior into a human, allowing
our minds to shift the lens.

The human emerged from the tunnel, safe and
sound,
And embraced the beauty instead of hovering
over the fiery thorns all around.

Is this a silent storm in our ribcage caused by
fiery thorns in life,
Or a war that cracks the hourglass, shaking
our strong grip over time?
Perhaps the lesson isn't in fighting battles to
conquer every disease in the end,
But to embrace all the good and bad in our
heart to truly heal and mend.

AS WE FADE AWAY

Ride or die, live your life because this is just
the beginning.
Ideas gleam in your eyes—do you see a future
where you're winning?
When Shakespeare said, "Life is a stage," the
world was busy looking for ceilings,
Yet dreams persist like forbidden whispers,
defying life's fleeting dealings.

The clock ticks loud; one of us fades away, like
petals falling from a wilting rose.
Time's endless march leaves its footprints,
weaving tales of life's highs and lows.
Wrinkles grow; some try to take it slow, but
do they really know
That finding some meaning in life before
fading can be the greatest way to grow?

The scars and smiles are ephemeral, but we
try to find our place in paths unknown.
When we fade to dust, we leave traces of our
dreams, as the seeds of our essence are sown.

FRAGMENTS OF US

A new generation rises to a challenging start,
We may not follow the norms, but we always
follow our heart.
We live in a world bound by conventions as
we defy the rest,
We seek freedom from all, to truly live and
express.

Our childhood whispers the wisdom of an
imaginary friend,
Those were the days when our mind could
guide us till the end.

As time passed by, a question lingered in my
heart,
Do we truly live, or merely exist to play our
part?

Through fleeting moments, many reasons to
smile we find,
To look for ways to tame a loud and
tumultuous mind.
As time evolves, some modern love stories
unfold,
With newer traditions, mutual respect
becomes the mould.

Mothers are the silent architects with lives to
weave,
They are hidden in shadows; bearing grief
they can't relieve.
"Take your time!" is the silent whisper of a
busy mind,
The train of life will find different ways to be
kind.

Focus on conquering fear of what others will
think,
Even a failure can be a judge, so cut free from
society's brink.
There are simple joys in life, like a hot
chocolate's embrace;
The warmth will give you the strength to
focus on every goal you chase.

Through the power of tailored love and
long-distance connections,
We find different ways to rewrite old bonds
with new dimensions.
But this journey isn't easy as some friends are
always left behind,
As we start to ponder over the question:
"Does wealth measure love in kind?"

Sometimes it becomes important to take a
break and breathe,
When the reservoir of mind allows itself to
grow beneath.

In its depths, a lazy sloth will linger, but
eventually meaning will bloom,
Because some patience and effort can dispel
uncertainty's gloom.

The uncertainty of life can always test us with
fire,
When dreams of ambition cross their paths to
conspire.
Yet hope is the constant anchor that gives
strength to prevail,
Even when the winds of life batter and wail.

The heart yearns for realistic yet honest love,
so pure,
A bond that's resilient even when life isn't so
steady and sure.
"You're beautiful," whispers the mirror's truth,
Each line is a story, a testament of youth.

We battle the pangs of envy within us; it's a
human flaw.
Learning to celebrate the success of others has
been life's deeper law.

The realistic world demands the courage to
toil hard and stay,
When believing in ourselves against flaws
becomes the only way.

A tick on the checklist of age-– is that really
all we can be?
Is there a perfect age to do everything as we
try to define our destiny?
Success is a journey; don't be distracted
before reaching the end,
As its roots grow deeper to deal with storms
that descend.

Reflections of our destiny can stare us in the
face,
As leaving behind our nests becomes an
essential phase.
Change is the constant, an imperative phase
we embrace,
As the precious dreams of a child fuel life's
endless chase.

The warrior within redefines her might;
The journey through the dark tunnel is not
just a fight.
To receive blame for a disease— is it a right
thought this time?
When life's a bundle of bittersweet moments
on stairs to climb.

In the end, we all fade away as only our legacy
remains,
There are many hearts we've touched, with
love unrestrained.
These are few of the many fragments of us;
they are scattered yet whole,
As the different parts tell the story of life
peeping into the depths of our soul.